Thomas Downing

New York's Oyster King

THOMAS DOWNING

New York's Oyster King

JOANNE REITANO

CONTENTS

Acknowledgments

This book has been a family affair. Adam provided technical advice, adjusted the portrait and adapted the map. Paul reviewed for style and presentation. Bobbi Jo checked the clarity and accuracy of the glossary, especially the scientific terms. Karlie sharpened the marketing material. Elliot (age 10) offered thoughtful reactions and suggestions. Anabelle (age 8) and Charles (age 6) assessed the images. All strengthened the book. They are special.

I also benefitted from the support and constructive editing provided by Ruth Benn, Pam Bolen, Clare Nolen, and Larry Rushing. It was a pleasure to work with Christine Horner of Open Book Design on the cover and interior layout for the paperback and eBook. She was consistently cheerful, cooperative, and creative. Although I do not know him, I am indebted to Mark Kurlansky for his important and engaging work, *The Big Oyster: History on the Half Shell* (NY: Penguin, 2006).

I hope that you enjoy reading this book as much as I enjoyed writing it.

CHAPTER I

INTRODUCING THOMAS DOWNING, Oyster King

New York was once the world capital of oysters and Thomas Downing (1819-1866) was New York's Oyster King. The only known drawing of Downing tells us a lot about him. Holding his head high, he seems serious, dignified, determined, and proud. He should have been because Downing was one of New York's most prominent, most successful early 19th-century men. Indeed, in 1857, the *New York Herald* called him "the great oysterman" and asked, "Who has not heard of him?"[1]

The son of freed slaves, Downing rose from collecting oysters to selling them out of a cellar to running the most elegant oyster restaurant in the city. He was considered "a commanding figure [with] kingly bearing... and manly character." Downing used his stature and wealth to help others by fighting for equality. Honesty, hard work, generosity, and good deeds earned him respect from black and white alike. His story is remarkable and inspiring.[2]

Downing had a head start because, in 1791, he was born free in the slave state of Virginia. His parents' "master," a planter named John Downing, was moved by a preacher who said that Methodists should never own slaves because slavery was cruel and violated Christianity. Accordingly, John Downing *manumitted* (voluntarily freed) his slaves in 1783, including Thomas's parents. John Downing then built a Methodist Meeting House and hired Thomas's parents to take care of it. He also paid for Thomas to be tutored along with the local wealthy white children. This was a bold move in a slave state where educating black children was rare, but not forbidden.

Although there is little information about Thomas's parents, we know that they worked hard and earned enough money to buy some land (maybe from John Downing) on the eastern shore of Virginia by Chesapeake Bay. They built a modest home near the meeting house where they welcomed upper-class white worshippers after Sunday services. Little Thomas played with their children and developed a lifelong friendship with Virginia's future governor, Henry A. Wise (1806-1876).

Growing up, Thomas learned from his parents the importance of being honest, working hard, and helping others. On the farm, he raised chickens and grew vegetables to feed the family and sell at the local market. Because the family's land was near Chesapeake Bay, Thomas knew how to row and sail a boat, fish and dig for clams. Chesapeake Bay was famous for its many large, tasty oysters and Thomas especially enjoyed oystering.

FOOD FOR THOUGHT: PEARLS

You have a 1 in 10,000 chance of finding a pearl in an oyster. Pearls are the oyster's reaction to something foreign that enters its shell, like a parasitic drill worm. If it cannot get rid of the intruder, the oyster covers it with a chemical coating that builds over time. It can take six months to get a little pearl, four to seven years for a big one.

Therefore, the older oysters, which are deeper down in the ocean and harder to get, produce the biggest natural pearls. Artificial pearls were developed in Japan. By cutting into the oyster shell and planting a grain of something inside, they tricked the oyster into covering it to make a pearl. However, the most desirable and expensive pearls are grown naturally, not artificially.

CHAPTER 2:

INTRODUCING OYSTERS

If you never thought much about oysters, you might want to ask some of these interesting questions:

What is an oyster?

Oysters are *mollusks*—soft-bodied animals often with a shell, like clams and snails. Oysters are called *bivalves* because they grow inside two (bi) shells (valves), which can open and close. One shell is fairly flat while the other is curved like a cup. It contains the oyster's organs—its heart, brain, stomach, intestines, liver, and *gills*. This body is what people eat.

The shells are connected by a hinge that enables oysters to open and close their shells. They open the shells to expose their mouths and take in water that contains the nutrients (food) they need. They close their shells when done. Amazingly, they can mold their shells in order to attach themselves to different objects like a bottle, a rock, a pier, a shipwreck, or any other surface. (*See* the photo after the Glossary.)

Where do oysters live?

Oysters flourish in *estuaries*, which are partly enclosed coastal areas where the sea or ocean mixes with rivers or streams to combine salt water with fresh water. Virginia's Chesapeake Bay and the New York-New Jersey harbor are excellent estuaries.

Many oysters clustered together make an *oyster reef* or oyster bed. As the oysters mature, they fuse together making a solid structure. The reef provides a safe, stable place for other organisms to live, including mollusks, fish, plants, and *plankton* (small organisms that oysters and other marine life eat). Oysters are the *keystone* (essential) *species* needed to create and maintain the diverse, balanced *ecosystems* that enrich our oceans, seas, rivers, and streams.

How are oyster shells special?

First, they contain the *calcium* that oysters absorb from the water. Calcium is an important source for the lime that goes into paint, mortar, and fertilizer. Oysters can even use their calcium to fix cracks in their own shells. Second, when discarded, the shells provide perfect places for baby oysters to attach themselves, grow, and create new oyster reefs.

Third, the shells of oysters, clams, and *conches* (large conical sea snails) are so pretty inside that Eastern shore Native Americans made small tubular beads, called *wampum*, out of the thickest purple and white parts. Strings of wampum could be presents, signs of status, markers of marriage, or messages of condolence. The beads could also be woven into clothing, moccasins, or pouches. Ceremonial wampum belts recorded key events and peace agreements. Wampum dating before 1510 has been found in New York State.

Native people valued wampum, but never over-harvested oysters. By contrast, when Europeans started using wampum as a form of exchange (money), they wanted more of it. To increase production, they increased oyster harvesting and introduced mechanical drilling tools. These devices replaced the old stone tools and enabled European women to make more wampum more efficiently by themselves. Consequently, Native women lost a key part of their personal identity and larger role in Native society. Thus began the exploitation of oysters.

What do oysters do for people?

Besides being a source of food, oysters are "the lungs of the ocean." Each oyster can clean 50 gallons of water a day. They get oxygen and food by filtering water as it passes over four layers of tissue called *gills.* During *filter feeding*, oysters digest good organisms and store bad ones in their shells. By keeping carbon, nitrogen, and phosphorous out of the water, oysters help fight global warming.

The marine life that lives around oyster reefs benefits recreational fishermen and creates jobs for commercial fishermen. In addition, the reefs act as *breakwaters* by literally breaking apart and slowing down the impact of big waves from storms that cause flooding, property damage, and loss of life. Oyster reefs can weaken waves by 76% to 93%.

How long have oysters been around?

Oysters are among the earth's oldest forms of life, coexisting with the dinosaurs. *Fossils* (ancient remains) of huge oysters three feet long and weighing over 20 pounds date back 500 million years. Fossils from a cave in South Africa show that people have been eating shellfish, like oysters, for about 164,000 years. They roasted the oysters over fires so that the heat would open the shells and expose the edible body inside.

Ancient Greeks and Romans served oysters at banquets to prove their wealth and status. They *farmed,* or cultivated, oysters by piling broken pieces of pottery or rocks in rivers as places for baby oysters to attach themselves and grow (*spats*). In addition, the Romans built special channels to guide salt water over the oysters and stimulate their growth. Huge piles of oyster shells and other refuse, called *middens,* were found on the bottom of the Mediterranean Sea. They prove that the Greeks and Romans ate lots of oysters.

Native Americans left similar middens along the shores

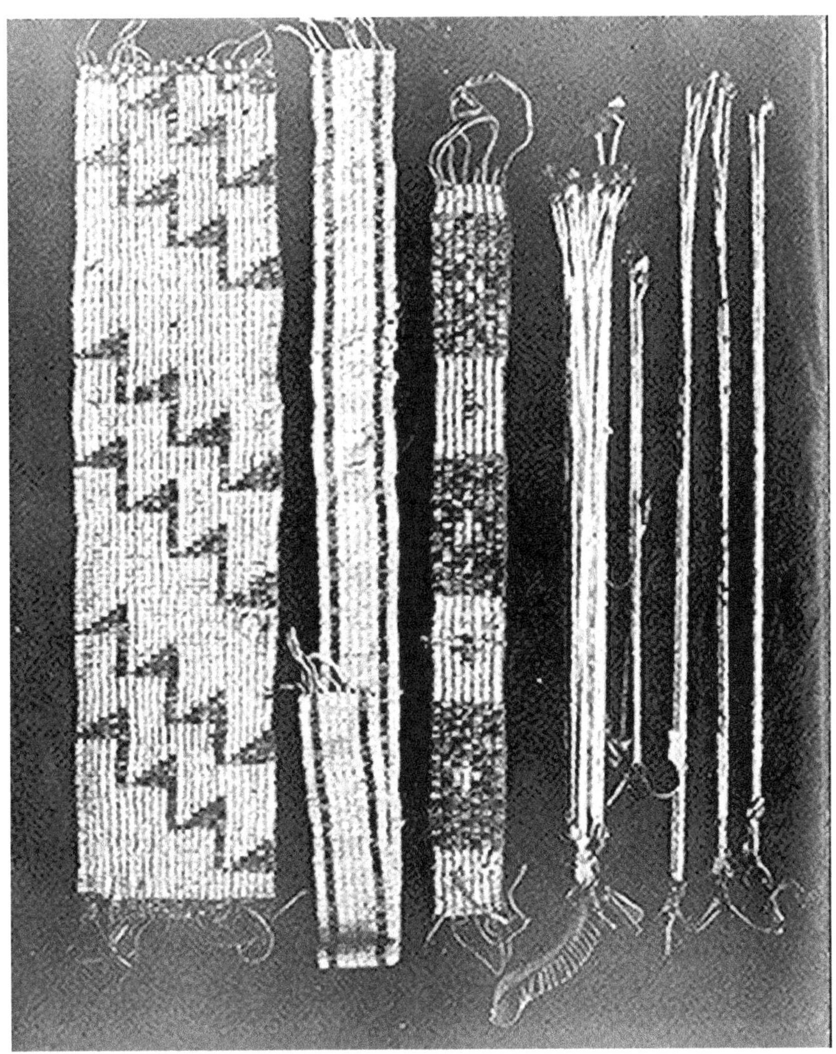

This museum collection reflects the Native American skill and artistry involved in making wampum strings of beads and wampum belts.

of New York and New Jersey. Some dated back to 6950 B.C. Many middens lasted until the late 19th century when the shells were used for construction material and landfill. There are still two old towns in southern New Jersey called Shell

Pile and Bivalve. They are national historic sites with old middens, an education center, and a museum about oystering.

Oystering was a field open to African American men. This drawing shows a large skiff in Chesapeake Bay. The man facing front is using tongs to surround and capture the oysters. The man behind him is dropping oysters from his tongs into a shallow trough (wooden container) where a boy is opening them with a wooden hammer. Some free blacks, like the man sitting down, made enough money as oystermen to buy their own boats. More oyster boats are visible in the background. They underline the fact that Chesapeake Bay was the nation's largest estuary with the best oysters.

How did people collect oysters?

If they were close to shore, oysters could just be picked up at low tide and put into oyster baskets. Farther out, you needed a small, flat-bottomed rowboat, called a *skiff.* You also needed *tongs*, which were two 12-20-foot-long rakes with small baskets attached to the rake's teeth. The rakes pivoted like scissors. By spreading rakes apart, the oysterman surrounded the oysters. By closing the rakes, he captured the oysters so that he could raise them to the surface. Native Americans had to teach the Europeans how to use tongs. Growing up on oyster-rich Chesapeake Bay, Downing was skilled in tonging.

FOOD FOR THOUGHT: SHUCKING

Shucking is the process of removing oysters from their shells. After opening the shells with a small, blunt knife, shuckers quickly cut the muscle that attached the oyster body to the upper shell, saved it, and discarded the shells. Shucking also applied to removing the husks from corn or the shells from nuts.

The word "shucks" suggests something unimportant as in "Aw, shucks," or "It's not worth shucks." However, for oyster shuckers, it had great value. Shucking was a skilled job mainly performed by African American men, but some women and children shucked too. They were either slave or free depending on the place and time period.

Shuckers stood, sat, or kneeled 10 hours a day six days a week, opening the shells and removing the oysters. The best shuckers completed the process in three seconds. Speed mattered because wages depended on the number of oysters shucked.

It was back breaking work. In order to make it easier, the shuckers held contests or sang. Contests enlivened the day. Singing helped shuckers pace their work, gave them some control over it, and created a sense of community.

Hard as it was, shucking was better than working in the cotton, sugar cane, or tobacco fields. Slaves would sometimes pretend to be too injured for field work in order to be assigned to shucking. It was a way of tricking the slave owner. Consequently, the word "shucking" became linked to "jiving," or tricking people and making jokes. Later on, jazz musicians used "shucking" to mean improvising. It is not considered a bad word.

Oyster shuckers from Sandy Ground, Staten Island, NY, 1895.

CHAPTER 3:

INTRODUCING NEW YORK CITY

As a young man, Thomas went with the American army to Philadelphia after the War of 1812. There he met and married Rebecca West, a free black woman. After seven years working as an oysterman and in an oyster bar, Downing wanted more independence. Ambition led him to New York, the city of opportunity.

The New York harbor was an excellent place for oystering. As an estuary, it had plenty of bays, coves, and inlets where fresh and salt water mixed, which was perfect for oysters. Observing that the Hudson River (originally called the North River) and the Atlantic Ocean interacted at high tide, the native people called it "the river that flows both ways."[3]

In the 1600s, there were 220,000 acres of *oyster reefs* along the shores of Long Island, New Jersey, and the five boroughs, as they were known after New York City was consolidated in 1898. Oysters flourished in the Upper and Lower New York Bays, the East and Hudson Rivers, Jamaica Bay, Long Island

Sound, and Raritan Bay. (*See* the map.) The *biodiversity* of the New York-New Jersey harbor was "second to no other *temperate* estuary" and contained over 200 different types of fish.[4]

To the Dutch, who controlled the colony of New Netherland from 1624-1664, today's Liberty Island was Great Oyster Island and Ellis Island was Little Oyster Island. (*See* the two dots in the Upper Bay near New Jersey and opposite the red oval of Governor's Island on the map.) In 1654, a Dutch official in the city of New Amsterdam reported, "Oysters we pick up here before the fort. Among them are some so large that one must cut them in two or three pieces." Similarly, a Dutchman visiting Gowanus Bay found that oysters were "large and full, some of them not less than a foot in length." (*See* the curved shoreline entrance to Gowanus Canal on the map.)[5]

Unfortunately, oysters were too plentiful, popular, and profitable for their own good. When the English took over in 1664 and renamed the colony New York, oysters were already controversial. One problem came from the widespread practice of burning shells for lime to make the mortar needed for the growing city's new homes and other buildings.

In fact, many houses had one cellar wall open so that oyster shells could be burned whenever required for repairs. Fearing that inhaling the fumes was dangerous, the royal administrators passed laws in 1703 and 1714 requiring that all oyster shell burning occur outside the city.

A second problem resulted from economic competition and over harvesting. Food was wasted as more and more people collected oysters just to burn the shells for the lime market. Moreover, people were collecting oysters without permission from areas where they did not live. Throughout the 1700s, local authorities tried regulating such behavior by seizing boats and fining their owners, but the laws were ineffective.

An 1867 drawing of the unspoiled pre-industrial Gowanus Bay at the entrance to the Gowanus Canal.

The demand for oysters was limitless. Because oysters were so plentiful and cheap, they were the basic food for the poor. Luckily, you could get all you could eat for six cents under the Canal Street Plan. If you ate too much, however, the cook would add a bad oyster to send a message.

Oysters were not just for the poor. "Everyone here eats oysters all day long," claimed a visitor in 1851. Oystermen sold their catch directly to vendors with street oyster carts or to merchants at markets like the Fulton Fish Market, which opened in 1822. (*See* the map.) By the time Downing arrived in New York, the city produced almost half of the world's oysters and was considered "the world's oyster capital."[6]

In the 19th century, over harvesting became the norm.

During the 1800s, oyster carts, the ancestors of today's food carts, crowded the streets of New York City. There also were many oyster bars. Often called oyster cellars, they were located in basements, where it was easier to store the ice needed to keep oysters fresh. In the evenings, oyster bars would identify themselves by hanging out a red muslin balloon shaped by a wire frame with a candle inside. (Electricity came later.)

Oyster carts and oyster bars proliferated in poor

neighborhoods like the Lower East Side's Five Points. Built over an old swamp at the intersection of five streets, it sank and stank. Five Points was the nation's first slum. It epitomized every negative image of New York City then and now—filth, violence, crowding, disease, and crime. Accordingly, the city built its major prison there in 1838. When English writer Charles Dickens visited New York in 1842, he wanted to see the infamous slum, but dared not enter without a police escort.

19th century street scene in New York City's Five Points showing the crowded conditions, oyster carts, and an oyster bar. The street is cleaner than it probably was because there was no significant sanitation department at the time—only scavenging pigs and dogs.

For all its problems, Five Points was a useful starting point for Irish, German, and Chinese immigrants as well as African Americans. Close to work in factories and on the waterfront, the area was a stepping stone to success. Its residents developed a lively street culture through theaters, dance halls, politics, and oyster bars. Oysters were central to physical and social survival in Five Points.

Downing was hard-working, honest, reliable, ambitious, and skilled. His son later praised his "iron constitution {and}... indomitable perseverance." However, New York was (and remains) a tough city. Many other African American oystermen were already there. Many oyster carts and oyster bars already existed. It would be hard to stand out from the crowd.[7]

FOOD FOR THOUGHT: PEARL STREET

According to legend, lower Manhattan's Pearl Street (just below Downing's Oyster House) was paved with oyster shells. This story inspired an amusing poem by Arthur Guiterman (1871-1943). He immigrated with his parents from Vienna, Austria as a child, graduated from the City College of New York, and became a well-known poet.

Guiterman imagined that the Dutch settlers formed a committee to decide how to pave an old Native American path. The men "dreamed of all pavings that had ever been known/Block, corduroy, cement, gold, mortar and stone." While they talked, they drank New Amsterdam's excellent Dutch beer…

• • •

And dined on the oysters abounding of yore
In numberless shoals of our fortunate shore.
The bivalves of our fathers deemed worthy of praise
Were giants that mock these degenerate days.
For find me an oyster in bay, creek or foss
Today that will measure twelve inches across!

A fortnight they tarried to feast and perpend
Surveying the road from beginning to end.
Then, lo! What a mountain of labor was saved
For even as they feasted, the road had been paved.
And paved for the tread of a prince or an earl
With oyster shell brilliant in mother of pearl.
So, "pearl" was the name undeniably meet
The burghers bestowed on that marvelous street.

T'was thus that our city's progenitors showed
The very best method of paving a road:
Appoint a committee to dally and doubt
And somehow the matter will work itself out.
So, taught by experience, that is the way
We manage the streets of the city today.[8]

CHAPTER 4:

STARTING

Downing began by buying a skiff. He got up at 2 am and rowed out to the oyster beds before other oystermen. Using tongs, he gathered the biggest oysters, opened a few with a shucking knife, and tasted them. Then he collected the best batch. With his bags full, he rowed back to lower Manhattan. Downing sold his oysters from the front room of the two cellar rooms that the couple rented downtown. Soon, he became known for having the tastiest oysters around.

By 1825, Downing has saved enough money to open his first oyster cellar. Like the others, it offered oysters raw or roasted. Business was so good that, two years later, he moved to a larger space at Broad and Wall Streets (*See* the map.) By 1835, he was able to rent the basements of the two buildings on either side. One expanded his dining area. The other held a large *vault*, or container, for storing oysters. At high tide, a spring running through the vault covered the oysters with salty ocean water that preserved them for weeks.

Now too busy to tong himself, Downing rose at midnight and went down to the docks in order to be the first buyer and select the best oysters from the oyster boats. He always made a point of paying high prices for oysters, instead of bargaining them down. As a result, he developed strong friendships with the oyster captains. Sometimes, he rented a skiff to get to the oyster boats before they reached shore. He bought the biggest oysters and put the oyster bags into the skiff.

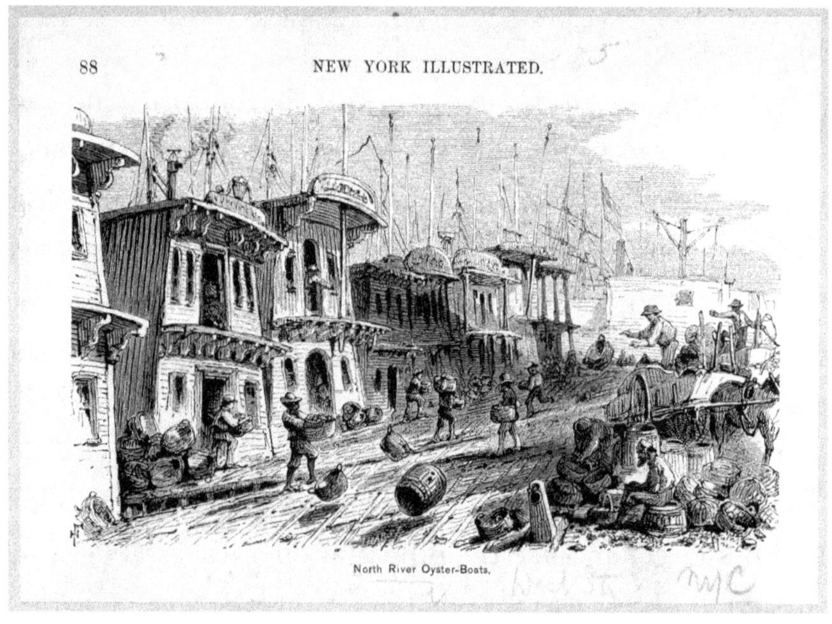

This 1885 drawing captured the hectic nature of the oyster trade in 19th century New York City. Could the man on the boat be delivering non-oyster goods in the barrels while throwing down empty baskets to be filled with oysters stored in the buildings? Could the black and white workers be returning the full baskets to the ship for delivery elsewhere? Are the two front right figures sorting oysters? The many ship masts in the background reflected the busy harbor. All this activity underlined the city's role as the nation's trading center and oyster supplier.

Then he returned to Manhattan and tied up the skiff away from the oyster auction market. Walking there, he waited for the selling to begin and offered to buy the smaller oysters that he did not really want. However, his bid pushed up the price and the captains profited. Downing treated them well when they came to his restaurant and they made sure that he always got the best oysters.

As a side business, Downing teamed up with an Englishman who wanted the calcium in oyster shells to make lime for whitewash. At first, their workers only painted walls, but they soon expanded to cleaning carpets. The business was successful and gave Downing connections with New York City's upper class. To his son, it reflected "a young man of swarthy complexion who was moved by determination and skill in his young days and [showed] a resolve to succeed." From the start, Downing was a smart, industrious businessman.[9]

FOOD FOR THOUGHT: SANDY GROUND

Free black oystermen from Maryland often came to New York to sell their oysters. After Maryland passed laws preventing them from owning land and oyster beds, they decided to stay. Virginia oystermen soon joined them. Starting in 1828, a year after slavery was abolished in New York State, African Americans bought land in southern Staten Island, near Tottenville. There they created a community sometimes called Little Africa, but generally known as Sandy Ground. (See the photo of shuckers above and the map.)

The sandy soil was not good for farming, but it was fine for growing strawberries and some vegetables. More importantly, the site was within walking distance of oyster beds between Staten Island and New Jersey. Some of the best oysters came from Raritan Bay, named after the Raritan Indians who lived there until forced out by Europeans. (See the map.) The new oystermen joined the old Dutch, French, and English residents of Tottenville. Everyone got along. A handshake was enough to seal a deal. Oystering so dominated Tottenville's economy that it was called "the town that oysters built."[10]

Sandy Ground, developed into a self-sufficient community of 150 African American families who thrived from oystering, making oyster baskets, supplying and repairing oyster nets and tools. Growing strawberries and vegetables supplemented their incomes. The oystermen also used their skiffs to participate in the Underground Railroad by ferrying fugitive slaves from Manhattan to relative safety at their Staten Island village. In addition, they rescued blacks fleeing from New York City's 1834 anti-abolitionist riot and 1863 Draft Riot. (See the glossary.)

Sandy Ground declined when overharvesting and pollution killed the oyster reefs. Now a historic site, it remains the oldest continuously inhabited free black community in New York State and among the oldest in the nation. Like Downing, the people of Sandy Ground used oystering to build independent lives. They made the most out of their limited opportunities.

CHAPTER 5:

SUCCEEDING

Downing not only served the best oysters, but had the most elegant, most proper oyster restaurant. Ordinary oyster bars were rough places where single men hung out, drank, smoked, argued, and fought. Respectable people, especially women, would never enter them. In fact, the red muslin lamp hung outside oyster bars suggested that they harbored prostitutes.

Realizing that the upper classes had nowhere to eat oysters outside their homes, Downing decided to create one. Although New York City was *segregated* at the time, restaurant and catering work were careers open to blacks. It proved useful that Downing's childhood experiences in Virginia made him comfortable with rich white people.

Downing's downtown location, at Broad and Wall Streets, was ideal. Unlike the Five Points oyster bars, Downing's Oyster House had tablecloths, fancy plates, curtains, rugs, and crystal chandeliers. The setting attracted bankers, brokers, businessmen, merchants, politicians, and newspaper editors. They even felt comfortable bringing their wives, something rare at the time. From 1830 to 1860, Downing's Oyster House was a favorite, fashionable place for the upper classes to meet, do business, or simply enjoy fine dining.

Downing's menu differed from common oyster bars, which only served oysters raw, fried, or stewed. In addition to those items, he offered scalloped oysters, oyster pies, fish with oysters, and a specialty, poached turkey stuffed with oysters. As Downing's superb oysters and oyster dishes became famous, he became rich. In 1845, the New York *Daily Tribune* listed Downing's Oyster House as one of New York City's best restaurants along with Delmonico's, the elegant French restaurant.[11]

The next step was catering important gatherings for the government, banks, shipping companies, railroads, and other businesses. The most elaborate event was the 1842 banquet honoring English author, Charles Dickens. Former mayor, Philip Hone, who frequented Downing's, called the event "the greatest affair in modern times." Downing was in charge of providing the food for 2,500 men (Women did not attend public gatherings in those days.) The banquet required preparing:

> 28,000 oysters, 7,000 fried oysters, 10,000 sandwiches, 40 hams, 76 tongues, 12 floating swans, 2,000 mutton chops, and a variety of other items. Dessert included 2,000 meringue kisses ..., 300 quarts of ice cream, 25 ornamental sugar pyramids, and thousands of pastries... It took one hundred and forty men and

women three days and nights to prepare the food, which was served by sixty men…

For his labors, Downing earned $2,200, then a huge sum.[12]

One of few oystermen shipping abroad, Downing sent his pickled oysters by boat to the Caribbean islands and fried oysters to Europe. He supplied oysters for an elegant dinner in Paris and gifted some to England's Queen Victoria. She was so delighted that she sent him a gold watch in return. Downing had become "the great man of oysters." He was New York's Oyster King.[13]

FOOD FOR THOUGHT: PROMOTING OYSTERS

The following 1838 newspaper notice shows how effectively Downing promoted himself and his oysters. Using the formal language of the day, he was assertive and self-confident, but gracious and welcoming. With his personal integrity and reputation on the line, he advertised his oysters, his restaurant, and his shipping business.

Oysters–Oysters–Oysters

The above article may be had in their prime at Downing's. I take this method of informing my customers that I have a better stock of Oysters on hand at present, than I have had this season. The lovers of the above article can (I feel assured) be fully satisfied by calling at my establishment. It is with pleasure I say that I can give my customers a better Oyster at present, than I could at any time this season. Strangers who have any doubts as regards the superiority of the New York Oysters, have only to call and try, and be satisfied.

Thomas Downing, 5 Broad St.

N. B. I have a fine lot of Pickled Oysters on hand for importation.[14]

Shipping pickled oysters required a strong container that would not leak and could survive being transported by boat. This medium brown stoneware jar was what Downing used. It is the only known artifact from Downing's oyster business. The words read: T Downing, Pickled Oysters, No 5 Broad Street, New York.

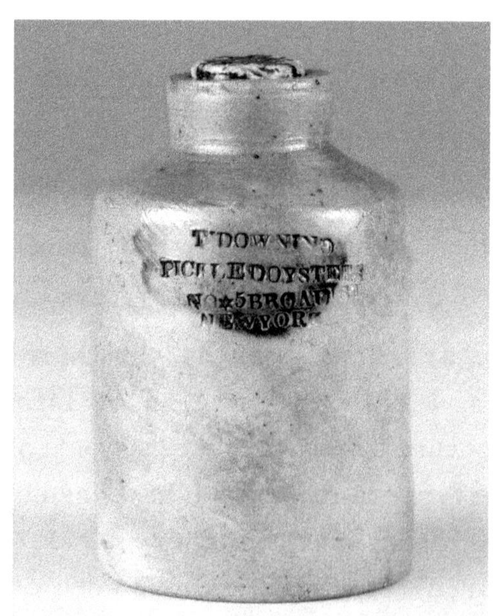

CHAPTER 6:

GIVING BACK

Downing's profits from his restaurant, catering and shipping businesses made him one of New York's richest men. Success and wealth were nice, but they were not enough. Downing wanted to help others. Above all, he wanted everyone to be free and equal.

Downing hired African Americans in his businesses and paid them good wages. However, long before integrated dining was acceptable, all Downing's customers were white. In this sense, he accepted *segregation*. But in another sense, he used his success to rise above and undercut it. Hardly a servant, Downing was a highly respected independent businessman. His status and wealth allowed him to fight inequality.

Along with other middle-class blacks, Downing supported several African American fraternal and self-help organizations including the New York African American Society for Mutual Aid. Formed in 1810, it supported members who were temporarily unemployed as well as their widows and children. He also gave generously to charities for poor people of any race. Downing even helped put out the city's huge 1835 fire by braving the bitter cold and throwing barrels of vinegar on the flames when water froze in the firemen's hoses. These examples reflected Downing's social conscience, activism, and community spirit.

SLAVERY

Slavery in the colony of New Netherland started in the 1620s when the Dutch West India Company began importing Africans as workers. After 1664, when the English took control, the Royal African Company increased the number of slaves. They were craftsmen, coachmen, household help, porters, construction and farm workers. Ironically, the wooden wall at Wall Street, which they built, had a slave market near the East River. It was also ironic that pickled oysters, largely harvested by African Americans, were part of the West Indian slave trade until Britain ended slavery in 1834. Slavery in New York State gradually declined after 1799, but it was legal until 1827, and New York remained segregated for many years after.

Downing was deeply involved in the struggle to abolish slavery in the South from the 1830s on. Although never seeking the limelight, he played important roles in funding and forming committees, calling meetings, and organizing rallies against slavery. In 1836, Downing helped create a New York African American anti-slavery society, which joined the larger, integrated New York Anti-Slavery Society three years later.

This famous 1835 image of a female slave praying for freedom from her chains was engraved by Patrick H. Reason (1816-1898), a renowned free African American artist. Patrick and his brother Charles L. Reason (1818-1893), a mathematician, were active abolitionists. (*See* the drawing of the school on page 35.)

The 1850 federal Fugitive Slave Act not only allowed enslavers to recapture their fugitive slaves from free states, but also required the residents of free states to help. In protest, Downing was a founding member of New York City's

Committee of Thirteen. It protected fugitives from being returned to their enslavers as well as free blacks from being kidnapped and sold into slavery.

The nation's first resistance to the new law occurred just eight days after it was passed. James Hamlet had escaped slavery in 1848 and was working as a porter in Manhattan while living in Brooklyn. After he was kidnapped and sent back to slavery in Maryland, whites and blacks jointly raised enough money to buy his freedom. When Hamlet was reunited with his wife and two children, thousands of people crowded the streets, cheered, and sang hymns.

Downing funded anti-slavery efforts and worked with other prominent African American *abolitionists*, including Frederick Douglass. With his respectable image as a cover, Downing turned one Oyster House basement into a station on the *Underground Railroad*. There fugitives could hide, eat, and rest before continuing their long, hard journey to Canada. Using legal and, when necessary, illegal tactics, Downing stood for freedom.

EDUCATION

Downing knew how lucky he was to have had a good education and made sure that his children were also educated. He and Rebecca had five children. George Thomas was the oldest, followed by twins, Thomas and Henry, then by Jane and Peter William. Sadly, Jane died young. According to George, his parents taught their children to be proud, "to stand up for their rights," to fight back if necessary, and to protect weaker children.[15]

In the 1830s, New York City had seven segregated schools for black children. They were run by the New York Manumission Society, which opposed slavery and opened the first African Free School in 1789. As a trustee of the New York Society for the Promotion of Education among Colored Children, Downing pressured the Manumission Society to fire a white principal who wanted blacks to go back to Africa and had punished a student for calling a black man a gentleman.

In addition, Downing's group got black teachers hired in each of the seven African Free Schools. They pressed for the creation of two elementary schools and a high school for blacks. However, because neither the city nor the state agreed to fund it, the high school closed after two years. Downing's actions were part of a broader commitment by African American parents to assert control over their children's education. Enrollment increased significantly.

Downing was a New York representative to the First Annual Convention for the Improvement of Free People of Color held in Philadelphia in 1831. While there, he worked on plans for a black college in Connecticut, but whites blocked it. Another setback was when the Public School Society absorbed the Manumission Society schools in 1832.

As a larger organization serving all children, educating black children was not the Public School Society's priority. Nor was it interested in parental involvement in curriculum and hiring. New policies downgraded the African Free Schools' level of instruction and fired most of the black teachers. The African Free Schools were now called Colored Schools, using the demeaning term "colored" and eliminating the important word "free."[16]

Black families were offended by these changes. Enrollment plummeted. African American parents who could afford it sent their children to a private school opened by a former African Free School teacher. Finally, the Public School Society woke up and sent a black representative to talk to the black community.

Some African American teachers were rehired, but the schools were not upgraded and the black community continued calling for better schools. Their resolve underlined their commitment to equal education, which did not become national policy until the 1950s. Yet, due to funding formulas, testing requirements, and residential patterns, New York City still has one of the nation's most racially segregated public school systems.

Downing often gave money to support the African Free Schools and sent his children to African Free School #2. After graduating, they needed private tutors, because there were no higher-level schools for blacks. Reflecting Downing's wealth and emphasis on education, he sent George to Hamilton College in upstate New York and Phillip to be educated in Paris. (The fate of the twins is unclear.)

Despite his privileges, Downing did not forget about less fortunate children and worked hard to get them a good education too.

NEW-YORK AFRICAN FREE-SCHOOL, No. 2.
Engraved from a drawing taken by P. Reason, a pupil, aged 13 years.

This image by a young Patrick H. Reason previewed his outstanding career as one of few African American engravers and lithographers.

THE VOTE

In addition to wanting New York City's black children to be educated, Downing wanted New York State's black men to be able to vote. Until 1821, they actually could vote if they lived in the state, paid taxes, and owned the same amount of land as required for white men. However, in 1821, the State Constitution was changed so that black men had to live in the state longer and own more land than white men.

Downing worked to reverse that policy. Along with other black abolitionists, Downing organized a protest meeting in 1837. A petition asking that all men be allowed to vote "on the same terms, without distinction of color" was signed by 620 men The state legislators were uninterested, but Downing did not give up. In 1839, he became vice-president of a new, more aggressive, statewide organization. Its members resolved that, "if one petition failed, another would be presented." Many such petitions followed.[17]

Their 1840 convention was held in Albany, the seat of state power. At the 1846 state constitutional convention, the issue of black suffrage was debated and rejected by a vote of 224,000 to 85,000. It failed again in two statewide referendums and at the 1867 state constitutional convention. Nothing worked until 1870, when the 15th Amendment to the U.S. Constitution allowed all men to vote, whether or not they owned property. It took another fifty years for women to get the same right.[18]

STREETCARS

Riding horse-drawn streetcars may not seem as important as slavery, voting, or schooling, but it was very important to people who wanted to get around without a private horse and carriage, which were expensive. Long before buses and subways, streetcars were the only form of public transportation. But the word public was narrowly defined. The horse-drawn streetcars were segregated and most of the cars were for whites. Only a few were for blacks and they did not run often. Walking was an option, but it was slow and difficult, especially in bad weather and for the elderly or physically challenged. Streetcars were daily reminders of inequality.

Photograph of a horse-drawn streetcar on Broadway.

In 1840, Downing got on an uncrowded white's only horse-drawn streetcar. As reported by William Lloyd Garrison's abolitionist paper, the *Liberator*, the agents "struck him under the ear... beat and kicked him" before they "violently forced him from the car." Downing sued for assault and battery. The railroad said that it always required blacks to ride outside in the back or on top of the car, but Downing denied knowing about it. In fact, he sat inside on his departing trip and only had a problem on the returning trip. Blacks often sat inside without incident. Nonetheless, he lost the case.[19]

Downing was involved in another streetcar dispute in 1855. One evening, he was with a lady who was in a rush. When they got on a white's only streetcar, the conductor protested and told them to get off. Downing refused and they sat down. The driver and conductor tried to get help from other conductors. Defiantly, Downing declared, "I don't leave this car until I get to the end of my journey... Gentlemen, if I have violated or committed a breach of the law, here is my card and you know where to find me."[20]

At that point, other passengers moved next to him and the lady to show support and protect them. Knowing that the driver would not stop when Downing rang the bell, he asked a white man to ring it for him. The trick worked. Downing and the lady got off safely and he filed another unsuccessful law suit.

Downing must have cheered later that year when Elizabeth Jennings won a similar court case after being literally thrown off a streetcar two times—first by the conductor and, after she climbed back on, by a policeman. An early Rosa Parks, Jennings was a 24-year-old African American church organist and teacher at African Free School #2.

Her young lawyer was the future U.S. President, Chester A. Arthur, who opposed slavery and discrimination.

Although other streetcar companies agreed to integrate, the courts allowed them to resegregate in 1856. A separate case led to an out-of-court settlement requiring one streetcar line to allow blacks and whites to ride together. Most, but not all, streetcar companies followed the ruling. Although public transportation was desegregated by the 1875 federal Civil Rights Act, the U.S. Supreme Court declared the act unconstitutional in 1883. Not until the 1960s was public transportation desegregated again.

RELIGION

Downing carried the crusade for equality to his church. He belonged to St. Philip's African Episcopal Church, downtown on Centre Street. It was the only Episcopal church for African Americans in New York. As a member of church leadership, Downing was a minority of one when the other members supported a bishop who had falsely accused St. Phillip's rector, Peter Williams, Jr. (1786-1840), of inflaming the 1834 anti-abolitionist riot. That bishop also prevented several blacks from studying to become Episcopalian preachers in New York. They included future abolitionists Alexander Crummell (1819-1898) and Charles L. Reason. Both attended African Free School #2, which Reason's brother, Patrick, sketched at age 13. (*See* his two engravings above.)

Later, Downing was in the majority when he led a campaign to permit African American Episcopalians to vote like white Episcopalians at church conventions. It took eight years, but blacks finally got full membership rights in 1853. Downing contributed liberally to rebuilding the church after it was damaged in the 1834 anti-abolitionist riot and the 1863 Draft Riot.

According to the 1855 *New York Evening Post*, Downing's character did not change after becoming rich. The only thing that changed was his ability to increase "the magnitude of his donations for the relief of his oppressed race." The more money he made, the more money he gave away. Downing's contributions to equality seemed rewarded when the 1866 Civil Rights Act granted blacks equal rights and full citizenship. His son, George, recalled that this milestone was the last subject they discussed. Citizen Downing died the next day.[21]

FOOD FOR THOUGHT: THE "R" MONTHS

In addition to reform work, wrote his son, Downing "made the nature and habits of oysters a study. He learned about the importance of the soil, the currents, and the tides for growing oysters. He observed that oysters were not in an edible condition during the months of May, June, July and August."[22]

Reproducing during summer made oysters small and watery. This was why people followed the old rule to eat raw oysters only in months with an "r." For example, in 1715, New York passed a law forbidding oyster harvesting from May to August. Sources even suggest that Julius Caesar may have created "leap year merely for the purpose of adding another oyster day to February."[23]

A second reason for avoiding the summer months is that bacteria grow in warm water. Oysters absorb the bacteria through their gills and can pass them on to people causing food poisoning or disease. That was the problem during the 1854 Oyster Panic, when cholera killed many New Yorkers. Although Downing insisted that none of his oysters were to blame, customers stayed away until the panic passed. Fortunately, today's health standards and food safety testing lower the danger. So do oyster farmers, who grow them in unpolluted water and keep them refrigerated. But people who insist on gathering raw oysters during summer often suffer the consequences.

Healthy oysters make healthy people. Adults who eat six oysters daily will get all the iron, copper, iodine, magnesium, calcium, zinc, manganese, and phosphorous that they need. In addition, oysters contain vitamins a and d, thiamine, riboflavin, and ascorbic acid. So, you can have your oysters and get your vitamins too.

CHAPTER 7:

LEAVING A LEGACY

Downing lost his lease on Broad Street in 1857 when the owner decided to rebuild. Because of his stature in the business community, he was able to relocate to the Merchant's Exchange Building on Wall Street. However, he was aging and decided to retire in 1860. His son George kept the business going for several years.

Thomas Downing passed away on April 10, 1866 at age 75. One of New York City's most prominent men, the *New York Times* and *Frank Leslie's Illustrated Newspaper* gave him full obituaries. The Chamber of Commerce closed for the day so that its members could carry the casket and attend the packed funeral service at St. Philip's. A long line of carriages was followed by delegations from his fraternal societies and scores of ordinary people.

These were exceptional tributes to someone who earned respect across the color line. The large funeral procession for his father was particularly meaningful for George Downing, Joined by "fellow-citizens from all classes," it reflected "the universal esteem of which he was held." It honored "the generosity, virtue and general goodness that was true of him…for he had a kind heart for all."[24]

Downing's example lived on in his son. As a boy, George led fugitive slaves to safety in his father's cellar. As an adult, he built his own restaurant and catering business in New York until moving them to Newport, Rhode Island. There he worked to get public schools opened to African American children and became a leading abolitionist. He helped recruit African American soldiers during the Civil War and fought for freedmen's rights after the war. Throughout his life, George Downing was dedicated to and actively promoted equality for African Americans. His father would have been proud.[25]

From a boy on the Chesapeake Bay to an oysterman, restauranteur, and caterer, Thomas Downing combined skill with intelligence and hard work to become New York City's Oyster King. However, he never let his personal success outweigh his commitment to equality for all. In 1854, an African American journal pointed out "that Thomas Downing, by his long standing and strict integrity, has proved himself worthy of, and receives, the highest respect of every man, colored or white, in this city and throughout the country, whose good fortune it is to know him."[26]

Downing's story proved that everyone can succeed if given a chance. Downing also showed how much good people can do if they think of others, not just themselves. Beyond wealth and prestige, he was admired for his reform work and for "the humility and modesty which [were] his most noticeable characteristics." Looking back on his life in 1887, the *Cleveland Gazette* called Thomas Downing "a remarkable character in the history of New York for more than half a century."[27]

FOOD FOR THOUGHT: "THE WORLD IS YOUR OYSTER."

Downing's life story fit the concept that "the world is your oyster." The saying came from a character in one of William Shakespeare's plays who declared, "Why, then, the world's my oyster/Which I with sword will open." The message was that each of us has the ability to achieve our dreams, conquer obstacles, and succeed. That is exactly what Downing did. He saw his opportunities and took them. His sword was made of skill, smarts, strategy, and social conscience.

CHAPTER 8:

LOSING THE OYSTERS

Downing's oysters provided lasting lessons. In his day, oysters were so cheap and popular that they were over harvested.

By 1820, the local oyster beds were producing fewer and fewer oysters. In order to renew the supply, *barges* were sent down to Chesapeake Bay to get baby seed oysters that could be replanted along the New York and New Jersey shores. The place where Downing first learned oystering as a child became the key to his success as an adult.

The replanting project worked. Although the new oysters were not as big as the old ones, they were big enough and plentiful enough to make New York City the nation's oyster capital from 1830-1860—the exact period of Downing's fame. The city became the world's major oyster trader and the center of an oyster boom with 700 million oysters produced annually by 1880.

Nonetheless, the oysters were doomed. Businessmen were replacing individual oystermen, like young Downing. Instead of skiffs and tongs, they used steam powered *dredges* that dragged a big bag or net attached to a wide, heavy wooden frame along the bottom of the harbor. The dredges dug deeper than tongs and pulled up many more oysters. In the process, they destroyed oyster beds. Moreover, they disrupted lots of dirt that spread over other oyster beds, clogging the oysters' gills and suffocating them.

Human waste created more problems. By the mid-19th century, New York City was dumping over 250,000 pounds of raw sewage into the harbor and rivers every day. In 1866, the city opened the nation's first water treatment plant, but it was a drop in the sewage bucket. Forty years later, the amount of untreated sewage dumped daily reached 600 million gallons. The resulting cholera and typhoid epidemics were originally blamed on immigrants, but were later tied to bacteria in the water.

Economic development made matters worse. On the one hand, because of late 19th century industrial growth, New York became the nation's most important city, second only to London in the world. On the other hand, industrial development created industrial waste. Without restrictions, industries dumped tons of poisonous chemicals into the harbor and rivers. As marine life died, progress became a double-edged sword.

The Gowanus Canal revealed how oysters were sacrificed to economic development. It was a 1.8-mile-long extension of Gowanus Bay on the western shore of Brooklyn, where marshland and salty water created a perfect place for oyster reefs to develop. Native Americans and Europeans praised

The photograph from Bivalve, NJ helps us understand the old system of dredging. It shows the large, heavy dredge frame and the nets used to capture the oysters when the boat dragged the frame across the river floor.

its beauty and its exceptionally large, delicious oysters. (*See* the drawing in chapter 3 and the map.)

Unfortunately for the oysters, the Canal was also a good location for water-powered flour mills and a convenient route for shipping goods inland. Over time, the area attracted more people, industries, and ships. In the mid-19th century, the Canal was widened once and deepened twice to promote commerce. By the late 19th century, about 100 cargo ships used it daily. The shores were overrun by mills and tanneries, stone and coal yards, paint, soap and chemical factories. Chemical run-off from these businesses polluted the water and the air. Raw sewage thickened the mix.

Tides could not clean out the water because the canal was closed at one end. Oysters could not filter fast enough to handle the constant flow of chemicals and sewage. Consequently, pollution overwhelmed the oxygen in the water. Without oxygen, oysters could not survive; nor could anything else. The canal turned reddish-purple and the bottom was covered in dark tar-like muck called *sludge*, also dubbed "black mayonnaise." During the warm summer months, sludge bubbles surfaced and exploded *methane* gas, which absorbed oxygen, trapped heat, and promoted global warming.

In the 1890s, the city built a new sewage system that actually created more problems by pumping sewage into the canal instead of removing it. As more people moved to Brooklyn, more sewage flowed into the canal until it looked like a Lavender Lake. A tug boat and a barge sank to the bottom, perhaps joined by murdered crime figures.

The pollution was so bad that, according to author Joseph Mitchell, "They used to tell about a tug that was freshly painted yellow and made a run up the Gowanus and came out painted green."[28]

Newtown Creek in the late 19th Century

By the mid 1950s, the Canal was being used less because trucks were moving more goods than ships. A pumping system designed to flush the canal failed and efforts to clean the bottom sludge were abandoned. The canal became a general dumping ground. Efforts notwithstanding, cleaning it remains a distant goal as governments argue, construction costs multiply, and pollution increases.

The story of the 3.5-mile-long Newtown Creek was similar, but different. (*See* the map.) A key shipping waterway located between Brooklyn and Queens, it was lined by tanning, metal, and fertilizer factories that dumped their chemical wastes in the Creek. Human waste created "sewage fed oysters." The stench was so bad that, in 1891, local people formed a Smelling Committee to investigate.[29]

Unlike the Gowanus Canal, oil refineries dotted the shores of Newtown Creek and added oil processing wastes to the overall pollution. The major polluters turned out to be companies owned by John D. Rockefeller. Newtown Creek oysters reeked of oil. Decades later, it became clear that the oil storage tanks along the Creek had leaked 30 million gallons under Greenpoint, Brooklyn, the now fashionable neighborhood.

It was one of the nation's largest oil spills. Moreover, the fumes from the oil and chemical sludge were rising through the water and the earth above into homes and businesses. A new term was created to describe this new situation. *Vapor intrusion* is still blamed for negative health patterns among Greenpoint residents. The fates of oysters and people were always intertwined.

In the 1960s, the city built the Newtown Creek Wastewater Treatment Plant complete with a nature walk. It handled most of the sewage and industrial waste from Manhattan. However, when it rained even a little bit, the plant overflowed sending industrial and human waste directly into the Creek. A later expansion was not enough to correct the problem. Today, the Creek's bottom sludge ranges from 15 to 25 feet thick, depending on the exact location.

The decline of oysters was cemented by land fill. The growing city needed more land and shippers wanted more piers. (*See* the map for piers jutting out along the shores of New York and New Jersey) All kinds of items became landfill on which to build more homes, businesses, and factories. When landfill covered the oyster reefs, they perished.

How could the city address all these problems? First, the city tried to ban dredging from certain areas. Then, it closed the oyster beds with the most pollution. Finally, it ended all oystering in 1927. Because similar patterns were repeated elsewhere, including Chesapeake Bay, only 15% of the world's oyster beds have survived. Oyster reefs are now considered among the world's most endangered marine habitats. Downing's oyster era was history.

FOOD FOR THOUGHT: FLOATING OYSTERS

The plumper, the better. That was the opinion of most raw oyster eaters. However, they did not know that their oysters were artificially "fattened" through "floating" or "watering." The process is exactly as it sounds. An 1887 recipe recommended that cooks:

> *Mix one pint of salt with thirty pints of water. Put the oysters in a tub that will not leak, with their mouths upwards and feed them with the above by dipping in a broom and*

frequently passing over their mouths. It is said that they will fatten still more by mixing fine meal with the water.

This was common practice for anyone preparing or selling oysters in the 19th century. The plumper the oyster, the higher the price.[30]

A similar strategy is used today, but now it is less about price and more about pollution. It also has a fancier name. "Depuration" is a method of purifying or decontaminating oysters. Mature oysters are placed in tanks with clean water pumped through it for two to six days. The salt level is adjusted to match the water in which the oysters grew.

By taking clean water in and pushing polluted water out, the oysters become edible. However, as an experimental depuration plant in Jamaica Bay revealed, depuration can only remove moderate amounts of pollutants. It is not effective enough for heavily polluted oysters. People living in those areas eat oysters grown or farmed elsewhere.

Depuration is also used to clean other kinds of shellfish, like clams. The method is supported by scientific studies and endorsed by the United Nations Food and Agriculture Organization These facts highlight how widespread marine pollution has become. Although depuration helps, it does not eliminate the real problem, which is pollution itself.

CHAPTER 9

RESTORING THE OYSTERS

If people created the problem, they could solve it by controlling over harvesting, sewage, and industrial pollution. Easier said than done. Industrialists resisted using their profits to safeguard the chemicals they produced or fix the pollution they caused. The city's efforts were inadequate. There were no national standards until the 1972 U.S. Environmental Protection Act made it illegal to dump raw sewage and industrial waste into the harbor.

In 1980, the Environmental Protection Agency (EPA) started selecting Superfund sites where pollution was bad enough to require that it be cleaned up by the polluter and/or the federal government. Both the Gowanus Canal and Newtown Creek became Superfund sites in 2010. However, the cleanups have been repeatedly postponed and both are still listed among the nation's most polluted waterways.

In 2012, Hurricane Sandy taught New Yorkers a harsh lesson. At the tragic cost of 125 lives and vast property loss, people renewed their interest in and appreciation of oysters. They knew that oyster reefs provide natural barriers, or breakwaters, that protect shorelines from strong storm surges and floods. They also knew that oyster reefs filter the water and nurture healthy ecosystems.

The Billion Oyster Project is an ambitious effort to recreate oyster reefs in all five boroughs. The goal is to plant one billion oysters by 2035. New York City restaurants have donated 2.5 million pounds of oyster shells for recycling as the foundations for new oyster reefs. The project makes citizen scientists out of 15,000 community residents who volunteer to help. In 100 New Yok City K-12 public schools, over 20,000 students learn about oysters and the environment.

Supported by the U.S. Army Corps of Engineers (ACE), the project also works with Rocking the Boat, a Bronx nonprofit that involves 4,000 youth and community members in boat-building, sailing, and environmental science. The program promotes STEM (Science, Technology, Engineering, and Mathematics) education and character development.

In addition, the Billion Oyster Project partners with the Urban Assembly New York Harbor School, located on Governor's Island. (*See* the red oval between lower Manhattan and Brooklyn on the map.) Public high school students get STEM education and train for seven maritime careers. They help build new oyster reefs by placing oyster *larvae* into oyster shells that have been cleaned naturally by the sun for a year.

The shells are then relocated to new underwater structures or *substrates*, which are made of special climate friendly *eco-concrete*. Once the larvae attach themselves to the substrate, the oysters are called *spats*. Spaces left between the substrate blocks become homes for plants, fish, and other marine life. Since the project began in 2014, over 120 million oysters were planted in 18 sites resulting in 16 acres of reefs restored. As part of the Jamaica Bay marshland restoration effort, 50,000 baby oysters were released with more to come. (*See* the map.)

The Billion Oyster Project and ACE supervise a state supported Living Breakwater project in Tottenville, Staten Island (*See* the map and Sandy Ground in chapter 4.) After 16-foot waves destroyed their homes in 2012, the community better understood the importance of oyster reefs for adapting to climate change and reducing the impact of storm surges. The project will revive the old oyster-based ecosystem of Raritan Bay by creating 2,400 linear feet of breakwaters and installing a floating oyster nursery. As the reefs spread and the shoreline is restored, Tottenville will become the town that oysters *rebuilt*.

A second Billion Oyster Project is in Brooklyn's Red Hook Shipping Terminal. (*See* the map.) Instead of the natural oyster beds that once enriched the shore, four big shipping containers served as oyster nurseries. *Gabions* (big wire baskets) full of empty oyster shells from New York City restaurants were lowered into 9,000-gallons of temperature-controlled harbor water in the shipping containers.

Millions of oyster *larvae* (immature oysters) were added to the water in the hope that they would attach themselves to the shells. When they grow big enough, they will be moved by barge to a new waterway, where they will be released to form new oyster reefs. The plan is to release 6 million baby oysters in the Bronx River at Soundview Park (*See* the photo and the map.)

A biologist with the New York District of the Army Corps of Engineers (ACE), places oysters in an artificially created reef off Soundview Park in the Bronx. She is helped by students from the New York Harbor School, Rocking the Boat, and other community partners.

A major problem is that sewage and rainwater still use the same pipes so that when rain overwhelms the pipes, sewage ends up in the harbor—27 billion gallons of it each year, including 250 million gallons in Jamaica Bay daily. Because of these Combined Sewer Overflows (CSOs), completely cleaning the harbor remains a distant goal. Cost estimates start at one billion dollars to fix the leaks in the city's aging sewer system and upgrade the existing waste water treatment plants.

The good news is that an 8-inch oyster was found at the Billion Oyster Project's restoration site at Hudson River Park off of 12th Street. The bad news is that many of the restoration oysters have not survived. Nonetheless, the harbor is slowly reviving.

As pollution is reduced and oyster reefs return, so do aquatic plants, striped bass, sturgeon, clams, mussels, and sea turtles. There are even reports of dolphins, porpoises, and whales. Above water, ospreys, cormorants, and bald eagles are fishing and nesting. People can enjoy the harbor again. Like Thomas Downing, the oysters are resilient and are defying the odds against them.

FOOD FOR THOUGHT: PEARLS OF WISDOM

"Pearls of wisdom" are brief statements that make us think about ourselves and our taken-for-granted worlds. They offer insights, warnings, or advice. Like the best, oldest natural pearls, they reflect the wisdom of people who lived many years, had many experiences, and learned many lessons.

For example, Tom Paine, author of Common Sense, the famous 1776 pamphlet, once said, "Man must go back to nature for information." Was Paine suggesting that, although we think we are so smart, we do not know everything and still have much to learn from Mother Nature?

Paine's pearl of wisdom applies to the story of oysters. We enjoyed them, but exploited them. The result was pollution, human disease, oyster decline, and shoreline erosion. Now, we are going back to nature for information on how oysters can build new eco-systems, protect us from storms, and provide us with healthy, tasty food again. It will be a win-win not only for oysters, other mollusks, fish, plants, and shorebirds, but also for people.

Ultimately, the most wisdom came from the oysters themselves. Although they were silent, their decline spoke loudly. Like Paine, they told us to value and learn from nature. Perhaps the best pearl of wisdom is offered by Native American elders who remind us that "We are all connected."

References

1 John H. Hewitt, "Mr. Downing and his Oyster House: The Life and Good Works of an African-American Entrepreneur," New York History (July, 1993), 248.

2 *New York Herald* (January 7, 1857) in Joanne Hyppolite, "Thomas George Downing (1791–1866)," *Encyclopedia Virginia*, April 25, 2023. (https://encyclopediavirginia.org/entries/thomas-george-downing).

3 Evan T. Pritchard, *Native New Yorkers: The Legacy of the Algonquin People of New York* (San Francisco: Council Oak Books, 2007), 21.

4 John Waldman, Heartbeats in the Muck (NY: Fordham University Press, 2013), 16.

5 Bayard Still, *Mirror for Gotham: New York as Seen by Contemporaries from Dutch Days to the Present* (NY: NYU Press, 1956), 10; Mark Kurlansky, *The Big Oyster: History on the Half Shell* (NY: Penguin, 2006), 81.

6 Kurlansky, *The Big Oyster*, 80-85, 113,184.

7 George T. Downing, *"A Sketch of the Life and Times of Thomas Downing,"* AME Church Review (April, 1887).

8 Arthur Guiterman, *Ballads of Old New York* (NY: Harper and Brothers, 1920).

9 G. T. Downing, "Sketch."

10 Askins, William, "Oysters and Equality: Nineteenth Century

Cultural Resistance in Sandy Ground, Staten Island, New York," *Anthropology of Work Review* (vol III, number 2, 1992), 7-13.

[11] New York *Daily Tribune* (October 7, 1845) in Hyppolite, "Thomas George Downing."

[12] Louis Auchincloss, ed. *The Hone and Strong Diaries of Old Manhattan* (NY: Abbeville Press, 1989), 104; Kurlansky, *The Big Oyster*, 212; Margaret Adams Highland, "Charles Dickens Dazzles New York and is Feted at the Glittering Boz Ball," June 6, 2023, mansionmusings.wordpress.com.

[13] Hewitt, "Mr. Downing," 239.

[14] *New York Herald* (March 30, 1838) in Hyppolite, "Thomas George Downing."

[15] G. T. Downing, "Sketch."

[16] Hewitt, "Mr. Downing," 241-242.

[17] Hewitt, "Mr. Downing," 242-243.

[18] Benjamin Quarles, *Black Abolitionists* (NY: Oxford University Press, 1959), 170-173.

[19] *The Liberator* (February 26, 1841) in Hyppolite, "Thomas George Downing."

[20] Hewitt, "Mr. Downing," 246-247.

[21] Hewitt, "Mr. Downing," 249; G. T. Downing, "Sketch."

[22] G. T. Downing, "Sketch."

[23] Kurlansky, *The Big Oyster*, 260.

[24] George T. Downing, "Sketch;" Carla L. Peterson, *Black Gotham: A*

Family History of African Americans in Nineteenth Century New York City (New Haven: Yale University Press, 2001), 388.

[25] S.A.M. Washington, "George Thomas Downing; Sketch of his Life and Times," Newport, R.I: Milne Printery, 1910.

[26] Hewitt, "Mr. Downing," 252.

[27] Hewitt, "Mr. Downing," 249, 252.

[28] Joseph Mitchell, *At the Bottom of the Harbor.* (Boston: Little, Brown and Company 1944/1959), 67-68.

[29] Kurlansky, *The Big Oyster,* 261.

[30] "To Fatten Oysters," *Housekeeping in Old Virginia* (1887) from FoodReference.com

PEMBROKE, MASSACHUSETTS

A. The Oyster Bar graciously shared its pearl.

Oyster Stew Grand Central Oyster Bar Restaurant

Shuck 9 oysters (March, 1977), reserving the liquor. In a saucepan combine the reserved liquor, 2 tablespoons clam juice, 1 tablespoon each of Worcestershire sauce and softened butter, ¼ teaspoon paprika, and ⅛ teaspoon celery salt, or to taste. Bring the liquid just to the boiling point over low heat and add the oysters and ½ cup half-and-half. Bring the liquid just to the boiling point, cook the oysters until they plump up and the edges curl, and transfer the stew to a heated bowl. Garnish the stew with a pat of softened butter and a pinch of paprika. Serves 1. ✤

101

Downing's famous oyster stew is still being served at Grand Central Terminal's Oyster Bar, which opened in 1913. His oyster pan roast with wine is available in the restaurant of the Smithsonian's National Museum of African American History and Culture.

Glossary

This glossary includes word origins because they are interesting, make words more meaningful and, therefore, easier to remember. Etymology is the study of word origins. It combines the Greek word *etymon* (true sense) with *logia* (study of). All non-English word origins are italicized.

• • •

Abolition: the movement to end or abolish slavery by government action. It comes from the Latin word *abolere* which means to destroy. If successful, the movement leads to freeing slaves by emancipation, which combines three Latin words—*e* means out, *manus* means hand, *cit* means to take. Abolitionists wanted laws to make slavery illegal. Thus, the hand of government would take away (throw out) the slave holder's "right" to own slaves. Abolitionists argued over whether emancipation should be gradual or immediate and whether slave "owners" should be paid for their "property" loss. Abolitionists were both black and white. (*See* manumission.)

Anti-abolition riot: The 1834 anti-abolition riot was New York City's most violent event until the 1863 Draft Riot. The riot started when white mobs broke up integrated abolitionist meetings on July 5, 7, 8, and 9. For twelve days, they fought with white abolitionists and destroyed their homes, businesses, and churches. In the Five Points neighborhood, they focused on African American homes, businesses, churches, and schools. No one died, but there was extensive property damage and general chaos until the state militia was finally summoned.

The 1863 Draft Riot began as a protest against serving in the Civil War. But it was also a response to President Abraham Lincoln's 1863 Emancipation Proclamation, which changed the war from a fight for union to a fight against slavery. Thus, white mobs attacked the homes and businesses of prominent white Republicans and abolitionists. Blacks were mercilessly assaulted including 18 men who were lynched and unknown numbers who were pushed into the Hudson River to drown. A black orphanage was ransacked and burned, but the children escaped. Although there were 105 known deaths, 1,000 people may actually have perished. Many blacks fled across the Hudson and East Rivers. Because the police were outnumbered, the riot raged for four days until stopped by troops returning from the battle of Gettysburg.

Bacteria: single cell organisms that were among the first life-forms on earth. They break down other organisms. Most are harmless to humans, but some can cause disease. They are used to make cheese, yogurt and medicines as well as to break down sewage and oil spills. The ancient Greek word *backteria* meant staff or cane, which was the shape of the organisms when scientists discovered them.

Barge: a flat-bottomed boat used to move goods. It comes from the Greek word *baris* meaning an Egyptian boat. In Egyptian hieroglyphics, the symbols for ba-y-r meant boat shaped like a basket. Could the final glyph be a boat?

Biodiversity: the variety of living species and how they interact in a balanced, healthy environment or ecosystem. It includes animals, plants, and other organisms. The term combines the Greek word *bio* for life with the Latin word *diversitas* for variety.

Bivalve: a creature inside two shells, as in the Latin word for two *(bi)* and for valve *(valvae)*, which is the movable part of a door, like the mouth of an oyster.

Breakwater: Large groups of oysters, called oyster beds or reefs, that support and strengthen the shoreline. Large rocks can perform the same function. By literally breaking up, or slowing down the impact of big ocean waves, the reefs or rocks protect the shoreline from floods. The Old English word *brecan* meant divide.

Calcium: a mineral needed for healthy bones, teeth, and body tissues. Oyster shells get calcium from filter feeding. It can be used to make lime for farming, cement, mortar, plaster, and whitewash. The Latin word *calx* meant limestone. It is also the word origin for chalk.

Conch: a large sea snail with an edible body and a conical shell that is good for making *wampum*. The term is applied to a variety of large sea snails. The Greek *konche* and the Latin *concha* both mean shellfish.

Depuration: the modern practice of using clean water to flush out the harmful bacteria in oysters and clams resulting from chemical pollution and human sewage. It comes from the Latin verb *purificare*, to make pure.

Dredge: a strategy for clearing out the bottom of waterways. In the 19th century, it involved dragging a big bag or net attached to a wide, heavy beam along the river bottom. The bag or net can remove oysters and plants as well as garbage and other dangerous materials. Today's methods are more sophisticated. In our daily lives, we often dredge up and bring to the surface, good or bad memories. Dredge may come from the Dutch word *dregghe*, which means drag.

Eco-concrete or eco-cement: an environmentally friendly substitute for concrete. It combines cement with natural or recycled materials and does not contain any harmful chemicals. Making it requires less heat than common concrete so it burns fewer fossil fuels and emits less carbon dioxide.

In fact, it traps carbon dioxide and provides a welcoming surface for marine life, like oysters, to settle on. The Greek origin of eco is *eikos* or home and the Latin origin of concrete is *concretus* or compact, condensed.

Ecosystem: when a variety of organisms live together as a community in a specific place, like an *oyster reef.* It contains living organisms like fish, mollusks, and plants, as well as non-living organisms, like water, dirt, and rocks. Its Greek roots are *eikos* (home) and *systema* (system). Similarly, the study of the relationship between nature and environment is called ecology, which combines *eikos* (home) with *logos* (study of).

Estuary: a partly enclosed coastal location where the sea mixes with rivers or streams to combine salt water with fresh water, especially at high tide. Its Latin origin is *aestus* meaning tide and *arium* meaning place for.

Farming Oysters: when oysters are encouraged to grow. It was begun by the Romans who provided broken pots and salt water to help oysters develop. Today's methods include spreading baby oysters over natural oyster beds or on artificial underwater surfaces (substrate). Alternately, oysters can be raised in wire baskets (gabions) or in special tanks. The science of farming oysters and other shellfish is called aquaculture. In Latin, *Aqua* means water and *cultura* means to nurture or grow.

Filter Feeding: when an oyster takes in water through its gills and digests the nutritional elements while storing the dangerous ones. Then, it pushes out the cleaned water. It can filter over 50 gallons of water daily. The term comes from the Latin word *filtrium* which was a piece of cloth used to strain impurities out of liquids.

Fossils: the ancient remnants of plants and animals that were preserved under sand, dirt, ice, or mud in the earth's crust or at the bottom of rivers, lakes, and seas. They can be shells, bones, hair, teeth, or imprints. The Latin origin is *fossilis* for dug up.

Gabion: a large wire cage usually filled with rocks, concrete, soil, or sand to build foundations for construction. If filled with oyster shells, it provides a substrate onto which oyster larvae can attach and grow. The word comes from the Italian *gabbione* for big cage.

Gills: People get oxygen from the air by breathing it in through the nose and mouth. Fish and mollusks get oxygen from the water as it passes over four layers of tissue, called gills. They sift out bacteria from the water, but save food, oxygen, and other nutrients. If water is polluted, the fish and mollusks cannot get oxygen and die. The origin of gill is unknown, but may come from the Greek word *khellos* meaning lip.

Keystone species: the most important species in an ecosystem. It creates the building blocks needed to develop a community of living and non-living organisms. As a keystone species, oysters are so important that, without them, the ecosystem falls apart. The term comes from architecture where the key stone is the top-most, last stone placed in an arch. It keeps all the other stones from falling out of the arch.

Larvae: immature oysters formed when oyster sperm fertilize oyster eggs in the water. The larvae float in the water until they find a place to attach themselves to ((spats) and grow into adults. The Latin word *larva* means ghost or spirit, perhaps because they are so tiny and float in the water.

Manumission: when slaves are voluntarily freed by their "owners," as were Downing's parents. It combines two Latin words—*manus* which means hand and *mit* which means let go. (*See* abolition.)

Methane: a colorless, odorless gas that can provide light and heat. It is used in industry to make other chemicals. Decaying materials in landfill, sludge, and sewage create methane, which greatly increases global warming by absorbing oxygen. It comes from the Greek words *methy* meaning wine and *hyle* meaning wood. The chemical was first isolated by charring wood and later by distilling wood (like extracting wine from grapes).

Middens: huge piles of used oyster shells and other refuse that resemble the Scandinavian word *myddyng* or muck heap.

Mollusks: soft-bodied animals often with a shell, including oysters, clams, and snails. The Latin *molluska* means soft shell.

Oyster: a mollusk or soft-bodied creature that grows inside two shells. It can filter water, digest bacteria, and trap dangerous chemicals. The word oyster is similar to the Greek and Latin words *ostreon* and *ostrea*.

Oyster reef or oyster bed: when a large group of oysters create solid underwater structures where other plants and animals can live and form an ecosystem. There can be almost 6,000 oysters (45 bushels) in a square yard of oyster reef with over 300 marine species living there. Versions of the word reef appear in several old languages, but the most useful one is the German word *riff* meaning ledge.

Plankton: small multicell organisms that drift in water like algae and some jellyfish. They can be eaten by bigger organisms, like herring, crabs, and oysters. Its Greek origin is *planktos* for small wanderer or drifter.

Segregate: to divide or keep apart people of different races, genders, ethnicities, or religions. It comes from the Latin words *se* (apart) and *grego* (group). By contrast, integration is when different kinds of people are able to be together in school, at work, on public transportation, and in other places. It comes from the Latin word *integer, meaning* whole.

Skiff: a small flat-bottomed boat with a pointed front and a square back. It can be steered by rowing with oars or using a sail. It comes from the Old Italian word *schifo* for small boat.

Shucking: removing the outer covering of oysters, nuts, or corn. For oysters, it involves using a small knife with a blunt edge to open the shells and cut the muscle that attaches the body to the shell. Its word origin is unknown. Could it be in Africa?

Sludge: thick, soft, wet mud that collects on the bottom of waterways. It looks like tar and is made of chemical run-offs from industries and oil refineries plus garbage and human waste. The term sludge may come from the Swedish word *slask,* which means slushy ground.

Spats: baby seed or oyster larvae once they have attached to a surface or structure. It is like the Dutch word *spat* for spot or speck. Spat is also the past tense of spit and one theory is that oystermen thought that spawning (when eggs and sperm are released) was like spitting. Therefore, the larvae had been spat. In addition, oysters seemed to spit out filtered water.

Substrate: a natural or artificial underwater surface to which organisms, like oysters, can attach themselves and grow. It combines the Latin *sub* (under) with *strenere* (to spread out).

Temperate: moderate climate that is typical of areas between the hot and cold regions of the earth. The Latin *temperatus* means restrained or between extremes. It also describes people who have mild or calm personalities.

Tongs: long rakes used for gathering oysters. The Old English origin is *tange* for fang or bite.

Trough: wooden container that looks like the Old English word *trog* for tub or basin.

Underground Railroad: not a real railroad but a metaphor of, or comparison to, a railroad. It was a secret network created by black and white abolitionists who provided safe places along the routes that fugitives used to escape from Southern slave holders. Borrowing from the real railroads, the safe houses were called stations, the people helping the fugitives were conductors, and the fugitives were the passengers. Because the system was illegal, it was kept secret and out of view, as if being underground.

Vapor intrusion: when fumes from underground oil and chemical spills rise up through the earth and seep into people's homes and businesses. The Latin meaning of *vapor* is steam while *intrudere* combines the word "into" with the word "thrust."

Vault: a large container, almost like a room. It comes from the Latin word for *volta* or roll because the Romans were the first people to use barrels with locks to store money or jewels. They also developed a system of curved arches called barrel vaults, to increase space within structures. In the 1800s, vaults were decorative stone rooms protecting graves from grave robbers.

Wampum: purple and white tubular beads carved out of the thickest parts of oyster, clam, or conch shells by Native American women. Working many hours with stone tools, they could only make one bead out of each shell. The unstrung beads were called *sewan*, a Native American word for scattered. It could take a year to make enough beads for a string of beads, which could denote status, marriage, or condolence. The beads could also be woven onto clothing or into ceremonial belts. The original Native American word was *wampumpeag*, which meant strings of white shell beads.

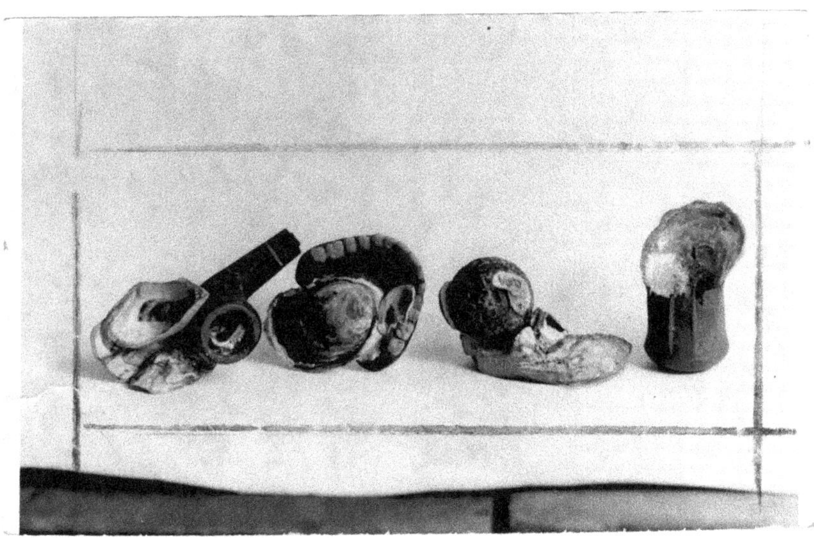

This photograph demonstrates the oyster's ability to attach itself to any surface including a pipe, false teeth, a golf ball, and a cap used to steady or reinforce something slender like a cane or chair leg.

Timeline

500 million years ago: Fossils proved that oysters were among the earth's oldest forms of life.

164,000 years ago: Fossils proved that oysters were being eaten in South Africa.

13th-9th century BCE: Greeks enjoyed oysters.

8th century BCE-5th century AD: Romans enjoyed and farmed oysters.

6950 BCE: Native American along the Hudson River enjoyed oysters.

1510: Evidence indicates that Native Americans were making wampum in New York State

1600s: There were 220,000 acres of oyster reefs around the New York-New Jersey harbor shorelines.

1624-1664: Holland claimed a colony called New Netherland and a city called New Amsterdam. The Dutch West India Company began importing slaves.

1664: England conquered New Netherland and renamed it New York. The Royal African Company expanded slavery.

1791: Thomas Downing was born free in Virginia to former slaves who were manumitted by their "owner."

1799: New York State passed a Gradual Emancipation Act.

1812: Downing moved from Virginia to Philadelphia

1819: Downing moved to New York City.

1820s: New York City began planting Chesapeake oysters in the harbor.

1821: New York State made it harder for African American men to vote.

1825: Downing opened his first oyster cellar.

1827: Downing opened his Oyster House.

1827: Slavery became illegal in New York State.

1828: The Sandy Ground community began on Staten Island.

1830-1860: New York City was the nation's oyster center

and Downing's Oyster House was its finest oyster restaurant. It made Downing New York's Oyster King.

1830s-1860: Downing was active in antislavery organizations and the Underground Railroad. He promoted education for African American children, giving the vote to African American men, plus desegregating streetcars and his church.

1835: Downing expanded into catering and shipping.

1836: Downing helped create a New York African American anti-slavery society, which joined the larger, integrated New York Anti-Slavery Society in 1839.

1839: Downing became vice-president of an organization promoting black male suffrage.

1840: Downing was beaten for riding in a white's-only streetcar.

1842: Downing catered the famous banquet for Charles Dickens.

1850: Downing was a founding member of New York City's Committee of Thirteen that helped escaped slaves.

1853: Downing's eight-year struggle succeeded when the

Episcopal Church granted African Americans full voting rights at its conventions.

1854: The Oyster Panic signaled the dangers of water pollution.

1855: Downing was harassed for riding in a "whites only" streetcar.

1860: Downing retired.

1866: Downing passed away.

1866: New York City opened its first sewage treatment plant.

1880: New York City produced 700 million oysters each year. However, commercial dredging and overharvesting were destroying the oyster beds while raw sewage and industrial chemicals were polluting the water.

1891: Residents formed a Smelling Committee to investigate the pollution of Newtown Creek.

1927: New York City banned oystering.

1972: The U.S. Environmental Protection Act was passed.

1980: The Environmental Protection Agency's Superfund program began.

2010: The Gowanus Canal and Newtown Creek became Superfund sites, but the cleanups were delayed.

2012: Hurricane Sandy underlined the importance of oyster reefs.

2014: The Billion Oyster Project began.

The Future: *It depends on us.*

Bibliography

Askins, William, "Oysters and Equality: Nineteenth Century Cultural Resistance in Sandy Ground, Staten Island, New York," *Anthropology of Work Review* (vol III, number 2, 1992), 7-13.

Billion Oyster Project, "History of New York Harbor," billionoyster-project.org

Burrows, Edwin G. and Mike Wallace. *Gotham: A History of New York City to 1898.* NY: Oxford University Press, 1999.

C. P., "The History of Oysters: Its Rise as a Delicacy and a Staple Food Beloved by Many," *Food Worth Writing For* (July 31, 2018). foodworthwritingfor.com

Downing, George T., *"A Sketch of the Life and Times of Thomas Downing," AME Church Review.* (April, 1887).

Guerin, Ayasha, *"Underground and at Sea: Oysters and Black Marine Entanglements in New York's Zone-A"* (2019). Shimajournal.org

Harris, Leslie M. *In the Shadow of Slavery: African Americans in New York City, 1626-1863.* Chicago: University of Chicago Press, 2003.

Hewitt, John H. "Mr. Downing and his Oyster House: The Life and Good Works of an African-American Entrepreneur," *New York History* (July,1993), 229-252.

Protest and Progress: New York's First Black Episcopal Church Fights Racism (NY: Routledge 2003).

"The Search for Elizabeth Jennings: Heroine of a Sunday Afternoon in New York City," *New York History* (October, 1990), 386-415.

Hypolite, Joanne, "Thomas George Downing, 1791-1866," in *Encyclopedia Virginia* (April 25, 2023) cncylopediavirginia.org/entries/thomas-george-downing.

Kochiss, John M. *Oystering from New York to Boston.* Middletown, CT: Wesleyan University Press, 1974.

Korfhage, Matthew, "Pearl of Virginia: Thomas Downing," *The Virginian-Pilot* (February 16, 2020) pilotonline.com.

Kurlansky, Mark. *The Big Oyster: History on the Half Shell.* (NY: Penguin, 2006).

Lamback, Briona. "The Double Life of New York's Black Oyster King," *Gastro Obscura* (September 28, 2022). atlasobscura.com.

Lobel, Cindy R. *Urban Appetites: Food and Culture in Nineteenth-Century New York.* Chicago: University of Chicago Press, 2014.

Mitchell, Joseph. *At the Bottom of the Harbor.* Boston: Little, Brown and Company 1944/1959.

Perlman, Daniel, "Organizations of the Free Negro in New York City, 1800-1860," *The Journal of Negro History* (July 1971), 181-197.

Reitano, Joanne. *The Restless City: A Short History of New York from Colonial Times to the Present.* (3rd ed.) NY: Routledge, 2018.

Richardson, Safari, "Finding Freedom Through Oysters in 19th Century New York," *North Carolina State University History News Blog* (February 18, 2019). history.news.chass.ncsu.edu.

Rockingtheboat.org

Rury, John L., "The New York African Free School, 1827-1836:

Conflict over Community Control of Black Education," *Phylon* (3rd Qtr, 1983), 187-197.

Sandy Ground Historical Society, "History," (sandygroundny.com).

Spillman, Rick, "Thomas Downing, From Son of Slaves to Oyster King of New York City," *The Old Salt Blog* (February 22, 2020). oldsaltblog.com.

Wade, Susan Elnicki, "The Rags-to-Riches Tale of a Chesapeake Oysterman," *Marina Life* (July 2019). marinalife.com.

Waldman, John. *Heartbeats in the Muck*. NY: Fordham University Press, 2013.

Washington, S. A. M. "George Thomas Downing; Sketch of his Life and Times," Newport, R.I: Milne Printery, 1910.

Wood, Stephen, "Pearls of Old New York," *Fraunces Tavern Museum Newsletter* (2023). frauncestavern.org.

Image Credits

<u>Downing's Portrait</u>

Schomburg Center for Research in Black Culture, Photographs and Prints Division, The New York Public Library. "Thomas Downing, New York City pioneer and restaurant owner" *The New York Public Library Digital Collections*. 1860. https://digitalcollections.nypl.org/items/8692940a-ff1b-1f62-e040-e00a180661b3

<u>Wampum</u>

"String and belt wampum, ca. 1890." American Indian Select List number 16, Native American Photographs, National Archives. https://www.archives.gov/research/native-americans/pictures/select-list-016.html

<u>Oystering on Chesapeake Bay</u>

Schomburg Center for Research in Black Culture, Photographs and Prints Division, The New York Public Library. "Mine oysters - Dredging boats in the Chesapeake" New York Public Library Digital Collections. https://digitalcollections.nypl.org/items/bcddb051-df19-1f90-e040-e00a1806337d

<u>Oyster Shuckers</u>

"Oyster Shuckers from Sandy Ground, Staten Island, 1894," Courtesy Alice Austen Collection, Staten Island Historical Society. http://maap.columbia.edu/image/view/806.html

Old Gowanus Bay

Charles J. Werner, *History of Long Island from its Discovery and Settlement to the Present Time.* NY: Robert H. Dodd, 1918.

Over Harvesting

The Miriam and Ira D. Wallach Division of Art, Prints and Photographs: Photography Collection, The New York Public Library. "Oyster shells for oyster "farming"." *The New York Public Library Digital Collections.* 1860 - 1920. https://digitalcollections.nypl.org/items/510d47d9-ab0b-a3d9-e040-e00a18064a99

Five Points

The Miriam and Ira D. Wallach Division of Art, Prints and Photographs: Picture Collection, The New York Public Library. "Midsummer in the Five Points" New York Public Library Digital Collections. https://digitalcollections.nypl.org/items/510d47e0-cd04-a3d9-e040-e00a18064a99

Oyster Trading Boat

Irma and Paul Milstein Division of United States History, Local History and Genealogy, The New York Public Library, "North River Oyster Boats," The New York Public Library Digital Collection, 1885. https://digitalcollections.nypl.org/items/ead71950-bb91-0132-1a5a-58d385a7b928

Downing's Pickle Jug

Collection of the Smithsonian National Museum of African American History and Culture, Object number 2019.52.

Kneeling Slave

1835 engraving of a chained female slave by Patrick H. Reason with the caption "Am I not a woman and a sister?" https://books.google.com/books?id=EzGVKN0BHFQC&pg=PA111

School

Schomburg Center for Research in Black Culture, Photographs and Prints Division, The New York Public Library. "African Free School, No. 2, New York" New York Public Library Digital Collections. https://digitalcollections.nypl.org/items/7f5929d2-994b-a2bf-e040-e00a180635d0

Streetcar

Irma and Paul Milstein Division of United States History, Local History and Genealogy, The New York Public Library. "Transportation - Trolleys - [Horse drawn trolley cars run on Broadway line.]" *The New York Public Library Digital Collections*. 1917. https://digitalcollections.nypl.org/items/510d47dd-a661-a3d9-e040-e00a18064a99

Dredge

The Miriam and Ira D. Wallach Division of Art, Prints and Photographs: Photography Collection, The New York Public Library. "Oysterman with dredge for gathering oysters, Bivalve, New Jersey" *The New York Public Library Digital Collections*. 1938. https://digitalcollections.nypl.org/items/17145a00-024c-0138-42bc-0733d6d87e1b

Newtown Creek

Irma and Paul Milstein Division of United States History,

Local History and Genealogy, The New York Public Library. "Queens: Newtown Creek - Nassau River." New York Public Library Digital Collections. https://digitalcollections.nypl. org/items/510d47dd-7711-a3d9-e040-e00a18064a99

Restoring Oysters

Ildiko Reisenbigler, ACE-IT, photographer.
Originally posted to Flickr by USACE NY at https://flickr. com/photos/40704398#NO5/5143311003. Licensed under the Creative Commons Attribution 2.0 Generic license.

Attached Oyster Shells

Photograph belonging to Frank Seerveld of Great South Bay, Long Island, 1938 in the *Brooklyn Daily Eagle* collection, Brooklyn Public Library, Center for Brooklyn History.

Map of the New York-New Jersey Harbor
Adapted by Adam Reitano

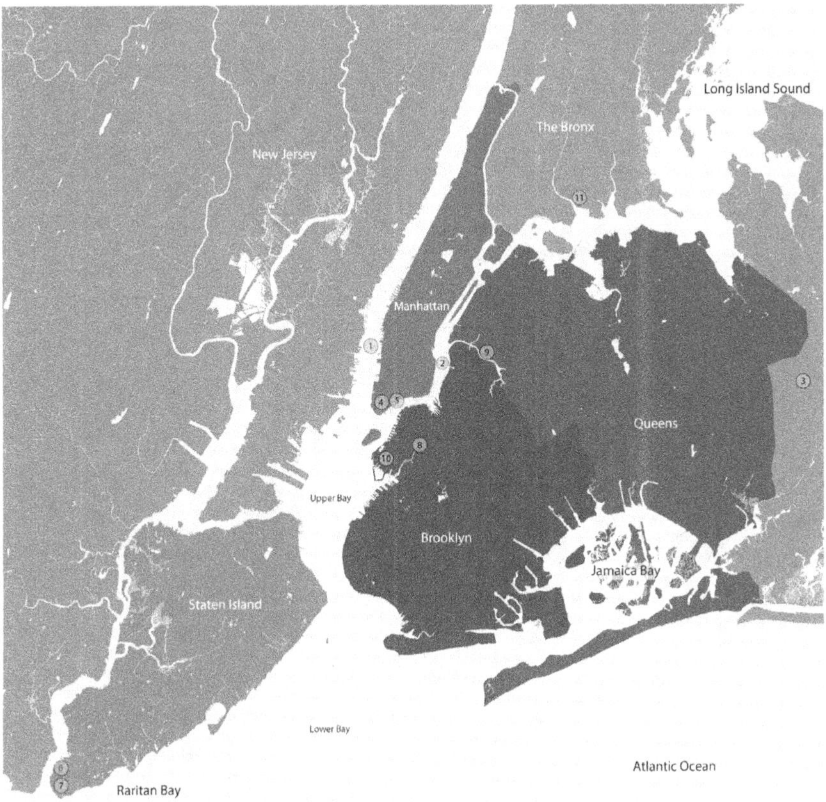

LEGEND FOR THE MAP OF THE NEW YORK–NEW JERSEY HARBOR

1. Hudson River

2. East River

3. Long Island

4. Downing's Oyster House

5. Fulton Fish Market

6. Sandy Ground

7. Tottenville

8. Gowanus Canal

9. Newtown Creek

10. Red Hook

11. Soundview Park
on the Bronx River